A GIFT FOR:

_____

FROM:

_____

Copyright © 2012 Hallmark Licensing, Inc.

Published by Hallmark Gift Books,
a division of Hallmark Cards, Inc.,
Kansas City, MO 64141
Visit us on the Web at www.Hallmark.com.

Editor: Jared Smith
Art Director: Kevin Swanson
Designer: Brian Pilachowski
Production Artist: Dan Horton

ISBN: 978-1-59530-481-0
BOK4148

Printed and bound in China

LoVe IS PATIENT, loVe IS KIND.

Inspiration from Corinthians 13

Hallmark
GIFT BOOKS

INTRODUCTION

The apostle Paul originally wrote this eloquent passage on love for a community rife with conflict, deep in dissension, to the point that its future was in peril. Paul had begun this community in Corinth (in present-day Greece) less than twenty years after the crucifixion of Jesus. Through his powerful preaching and teaching, people from all walks of life had come together to live, not according to the culture, but to follow a way of life based on God's love.

Paul loved this community. So, imagine his shock and despair when, two years later while in Ephesus (in present-day Turkey), he received word that his beloved community was in crisis. What happened? Instead of following Paul's teaching, the Corinthians had become arrogant about their newfound spirituality. They were living out of self-centeredness rather than being turned toward one another. And so he wrote a letter imploring them to get back on track and to start living on the basis of God's love.

Paul's message asserts the permanence of love, contrasting it with other spiritual experiences that are more transitory. He is convinced that at the heart of the world is God's loving desire for all people to know love. At the end of time, when God completes His good and loving purposes, nothing but love will matter. We won't need faith or hope anymore, because all will be fulfilled in God. We will remain in love with God and with one another for eternity. Love is the constant that endures from this imperfect world now until the perfect time to come.

Why have Paul's words endured for over two millennia? Perhaps because, in our hearts, we resonate with Paul's conviction that love *is* all we need—as complicated and as conflicted as that can sometimes seem. Love is a power, a force that is unfathomable, immeasurable, eternal and abiding. To love—to truly love—is to participate in God's love for us—a love that believes all things, hopes all things, and endures all things. No matter what life gives us, this love—God's love—never fails and never ends.

If I speak in the
TONGUES OF MEN OR OF ANGELS,
but do not have love

I am only a

resounding gong or a

clanging cymbal.

If I have the

GIFT OF PROPHECY

and can fathom

ALL MYSTERIES AND

ALL KNOWLEDGE,

and if I have a

FAITH

THAT CAN

move mountains,

but do not have

I am

NOTHING.

If I give all I possess
to the POOr
and give over my body
to HardSHIP
that I may boast,

but do not have

love

I gain NOTHING.

Love IS PATIENT,
love IS KIND.

It does not ENVY, it
does not BOAST, it
is not PROUD.

It does not

disHonor

others,

it is not

SELF-SEEKING,

it is not easily

ANGERED,

it keeps no record of

WRONGS.

Love does not delight in e

t rejoices with the truth.

It always pROtECTs,
always trUSts,

always hopes,
always perseveres.

Love neVer fAils.

But where there are prophecies,

THEY WILL cease;

where there are tongues,

THEY WILL BE STILLED;

where there is knowledge,

it will PASS AWAY.

For we know

IN PART

and we prophesy

IN PART,

but when

COMPLETENESS

comes,

what is in part

DISAPPEARS.

When I was a child,

I talkEd

like a child,

I thOUGhT

like a child,

I rEASONeD

like a child.

When I became a man,

I put the ways of childhood

BEHIND ME.

For now we see only a reflection

as in a mirror;

then we shall see

fACE to faCe.

Now I know in pa

en shall I

know fully

even as I am

fully known.

And now these three remain:

fAitH
hoPe
and
loVE.

But the greatest of these is

If you have enjoyed this book

or it has touched your life in some way,

Hallmark would love to hear from you.

Please send comments to:

Book Feedback, Hallmark Cards, Inc.

2501 McGee Street, Mail Drop 215

Kansas City, MO 64108

Or e-mail us at:

booknotes@hallmark.com